My First Bible

Stories from the New Testament

Written by Katherine Sully

Illustrated by Simona Sanfilippo

SWEET
WATER
PRESS

402 Industrial Lane
Birmingham, Alabama 35211

Copyright © QEB Publishing, Inc. 2014

This 2017 edition published by Sweet Water Press by arrangement with QEB Publishing.

Published in the United States by QEB Publishing
Part of The Quarto Group
6 Orchard, Lake Forest, CA 92630

A CIP record for this book is available from the Library of Congress.

Consultant: Fiona Moss, RE Adviser at RE Today Services
Editor: Cathy Jones
Designer: Chris Fraser
QED Project Editor: Tasha Percy
Managing Editor: Victoria Garrard
Design Manager: Anna Lubecka

ISBN: 978 1 49241 632 6

Printed in China

CONTENTS

The Birth of Jesus

Long ago, in the town of
Nazareth, lived a young
woman called Mary.
One day, Mary had a shock
—she saw an angel.

The angel Gabriel said,
"Don't be afraid,
I bring you good news
about Christ our Lord,
the king of the Jews.

"God is going to bless you with a baby,"
said Gabriel. "His name will be Jesus."

"I will do as God asks," said Mary.

Now, Mary was engaged to marry Joseph, the carpenter. What would he think about Mary having a baby?

Joseph was upset. But then, one night, he had a dream. In his dream an angel told him all about Mary's baby coming from God.

"You will name the baby Jesus," said the angel.
When Joseph woke up, he understood.

So Joseph and Mary were married.

At this time, everyone had to be counted so that they could pay taxes. Mary and Joseph had to go to Joseph's home town to be counted.

Mary was pregnant and almost ready to have her baby. So she rode on a donkey. It was a long, tiring journey.

They traveled all the way from Nazareth to Bethlehem.

When, at last, Mary
and Joseph arrived in
Bethlehem, the streets
were crowded.

There was no room left at the inn.

What could they do?
Where could they stay?

Joseph found a stable and
Mary settled down in the straw.

That night, baby Jesus was born in the stable.
Mary rocked the baby in her arms.

Neigh!

Moo!

Baa!

Cluck!

Cluck!

Baa!

Then she wrapped him in blankets and laid him gently in a manger of hay.

Moo!

Hee-haw!

The same night, some shepherds were looking after their sheep.

Baa!

Suddenly, they were afraid.
A crowd of singing angels appeared in the sky.

Baa!

"Don't be afraid,
I bring you good news
about Christ our Lord,
the king of the Jews,"
sang an angel.
"You will find him in a manger."

Baa!

Baa!

Baa!

17

The shepherds hurried to
Bethlehem to see if it was true.

And it was true!
They found baby Jesus
lying in a manger.

The shepherds thanked God and went
to tell everyone their story.

Far from Bethlehem, three wise men from the east saw a bright star in the night sky.

The star was a sign
—a new king of the
Jews had been born.

They set off on a long
journey to Jerusalem
to see King Herod.
He would know all about it!

"Where is the new king?" the wise men asked King Herod.

King Herod knew nothing about it! He asked his advisers where this new king had been born.

"In Bethlehem, so it is told," they said.
So King Herod sent the wise men to Bethlehem.

"Tell me when you find him," said King Herod.
He didn't want anyone else to be king.

The three wise men followed the star to Bethlehem
until it shone above a house.

The wise men found Mary and Jesus
inside the house.

They bowed down and gave him
gifts of gold, frankincense, and myrrh.

In a dream, the wise men were warned not to tell King Herod where Jesus lived. So they went straight home.

Joseph took Mary and baby Jesus to Egypt, where they were safe from King Herod.

Next Steps

Look back through the book to find more to talk about and join in with.

* Copy the actions. Do the actions with the characters—rock the baby Jesus in your arms; bow down; follow the star.

* Join in with the rhyme. Pause to encourage joining in with,
  "Don't be afraid, I bring you good news
  About Christ our Lord, the king of the Jews."

* Count in threes. Count three sheep, three hens, three shepherds, three wise men.

* Name the colors. What colors are the angels wearing? Look back to spot the colors on other pages.

* All shapes and sizes. Describe the gifts that the wise men bring.

* Listen to the noisy animals in the stable. When you see the word on the page, point and make the sound—Moo! Baa! Cluck! Hee-haw! Neigh!

Now that you've read the story . . . what do you remember?

* Who told Mary that she was going to have a baby?
* What name were Mary and Joseph told to give their baby?
* Who was Joseph?
* Where was Jesus born?
* How were the shepherds told about Jesus?
* How did the wise men find Jesus?

What does the story tell us?
God sent us the baby Jesus to be Christ our Lord.

The Baptism of Jesus

Jesus had a cousin called John.
John traveled through the desert preaching.

He had no fine clothes
or food. His clothes were made
of camel hair tied around his
waist with a leather belt.

He lived on locusts
and wild honey.

Baa!

Baa!

Baa!

John had an important message
for everyone he met.

Bzzzz!

Bzzzz!

29

John told them, "Ask God to forgive all the bad choices you have made, live a better life, and it will lead to the kingdom of heaven."

"How do we do that?" asked the crowd.

"Come to the river today,
and I'll wash your sins away,"
said John.

Day after day, people came from far and wide to the River Jordan.

One by one, John dipped them in the river to wash away their sins.

"I am baptizing you with water," he said,
"but someone else will come after me who will
baptize you with God's love."
The people wondered who he could mean.

One day, Jesus came from Galilee to the River Jordan to be baptized.

"Why do you want me to baptize you?" asked John. "You should be baptizing me."

"I have come to the river today, because this is the right way," said Jesus.

So John baptized Jesus in the River Jordan.

As soon as Jesus was baptized, heaven opened, and God's love came down like a dove.

A voice from heaven said, "This is my Son, whom I love."

Could this man, Jesus, be the Son of God,
the people wondered.

After he was baptized, Jesus went into the desert.
For forty days and forty nights, he was
alone in the desert.

The hot sun beat
down and the desert
wind blew.

He had plenty of time
to think, but Jesus
had nothing to eat.
He was very hungry.

Then, the devil came to test Jesus with bad thoughts.

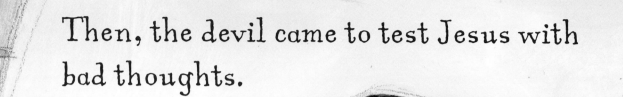

He whispered in Jesus' ear,
"If you are the Son of God, tell
these stones to become bread."

But Jesus replied,
"We can't live just on bread.
We need God's love, too."

The devil took Jesus to a high tower.

Then the devil whispered a second time.
"If you are the Son of God," he said,
"throw yourself off this tower.
God's angels will catch you."

But Jesus replied, "If we have trust in God,
we don't need to test him."

The devil took Jesus to a mountaintop.
For a third time, the devil whispered,
"If you worship me, I will give you
all the kingdoms of the world."

But Jesus replied, "No, go away!
We should only worship God."

44

Jesus pushed the devil away.
Then angels came and looked after him.

When Jesus came back from the desert,
he received bad news. His cousin, John,
had spoken out against the king
and had been put in prison.

Cluck!

Cheep!

Cluck!

Jesus remembered
what John had said.

Cheep!

From that time on, Jesus told everyone he met, "Ask God to forgive all the bad choices you have made, live a better life, and it will lead to the kingdom of heaven."

Next Steps

Look back through the book to find more to talk about and join in with.

* Copy the actions. Do the actions with the characters—pretend to sprinkle water on someone's head; pretend to flap your wings like a dove; whisper in someone's ear.

* Join in with the rhyme. Pause to encourage joining in with "Come to the river today, and I'll wash your sins away."

* Count in threes or fours. Count the sheep, the hens, the children.

* Name the colors. What colors can you find in the crowd?

* All shapes and sizes. Look for big, middle-size, and small sheep and hens.

* Listen to the noises in the story. When you see the word on the page, point and make the sound—Splash! Baa! Bzzzzz!

Now that you've read the story . . . what do you remember?

* Who was John?
* Why was he called John the Baptist?
* Where was Jesus baptized?
* What happened when Jesus was baptized?
* Who tempted Jesus, and how many times was he tempted?
* What did Jesus tell people that John the Baptist had told him?

What does the story tell us?
Jesus was chosen by God, and his trust in God was tested.

Jesus and his Disciples

When Jesus was a young man, he traveled
from village to village teaching God's message.

Wherever he went, people came
to hear the stories he told.

Soon, lots of people had heard about Jesus. Whenever he arrived in a village, a crowd quickly gathered to meet him.

One day, a big crowd followed Jesus down to the lake. There wasn't enough room for everybody, so Jesus asked a man called Peter if he could use his boat.

Peter pushed the boat
a little way into the water.
Now everyone could see and hear Jesus.

While Jesus was teaching the crowd,
the other fishermen were putting
their nets away.

When Jesus had finished, he said to Peter,
"Take the boat out into deep water
and cast your net."

"We fished all night and caught nothing," said Peter. "But if you say so."

Peter sailed to the deepest
part of the lake and
cast his net.

Soon the net was full of fish!
It was so full that the net broke.

Peter called the other
boat over to help.

As they hauled in the fish,
the boats began to sink!

The fishermen couldn't believe
how many fish they had caught.

FLIP!

Peter knelt down to thank Jesus, because he didn't
think he deserved it. But Jesus said to them,
"Follow me, then you'll be fishers of men!"

When they reached the shore, Peter and the other fishermen, Andrew, James, and John, left their boats to follow Jesus.

FLOP!

Jesus chose twelve disciples from his many followers:

Peter

Andrew,
Peter's brother

Philip

Bartholomew

James

John,
James's brother

60

Thomas

Matthew

James,
the younger

Thaddeus

Simon

Judas

"Follow me, then you'll be
God's messengers," said Jesus.

61

One day, Jesus told a story:
"Once, a farmer sowed some seeds. Some fell on the path where birds pecked them, some fell on stony ground, and some fell in the weeds.

"What does the story mean?" asked the disciples.

"The seeds are the things that God tells us. Sometimes people don't want to listen to what God says, like the seeds on the path.

Sometimes people forget what God tells them, like the seeds on the stony ground.

Sometimes people
are too busy to
listen to God,
like the seeds
in the weeds.

But the people
who listen to God
grow stronger,
like the seeds that
fell on good soil."

All kinds of people came to listen to Jesus,
even bad people.

"Why do you waste time on these bad people?"
Jesus was asked. He told a story to help
everyone understand.

"Once, a shepherd was looking after a hundred sheep. He counted them up to ninety-nine . . . there was one missing.

Baa!

Baa!

So he made sure his flock was safe and went to search for the one lost sheep."

"The shepherd searched and searched until he found the lost sheep.

Baa!

Baa!

He was very happy and carried it over his shoulders all the way home.

68

God is like the shepherd. He worries
for the bad people and is overjoyed
when they are found and sorry
for what they have done."

Next Steps

Look back through the book to find more to talk about and join in with.

* Copy the actions. Do the actions with the characters—haul up the fishing nets; scatter the seeds; search for sheep.

* Join in with the rhyme. Pause to encourage joining in with
"Follow me, then
You'll be fishers of men!"

* Count the disciples. Can you name all twelve of them?

* Name the colors. What colors are the fish? Look back to spot the colors on other pages.

* All shapes and sizes. Look for big, middle-sized, and small fish and birds.

* Listen to the sounds. When you see the word on the page, point and make the sound—Flip! Flop! Caw! Baa!

Now that you've read the story . . . what do you remember?

* Why did Jesus get into Peter's boat?
* What happened when Peter pulled up his fishing nets?
* How many disciples did Jesus choose?
* What happened to the seeds that fell on stony ground?
* What happened to the seeds that fell on good soil?
* Who found the lost sheep?

What does the story tell us?
Jesus chose twelve good men to help him spread
God's message.

The
Miracles of Jesus

Jesus loved to teach God's message,
and people loved to listen to him.

They followed him everywhere.

But one day, Jesus was sad because
his cousin, John, had died.
Jesus got on a boat
to rest and pray.

When he came back to shore, the people were still waiting for him.

Jesus welcomed them.

He started to teach and heal the sick people.

All day, Jesus spoke to the crowd.
When evening came, the disciples said to Jesus,
"It's late, and these people are far from home.
Send them away, so they can buy some food."

"You can give them some food," replied Jesus.

"That would cost too much!"
the disciples grumbled.

"Go and find out how much food we have,"
Jesus told his disciples.

The disciples went off
among the crowd. They came
back with a boy who had
five loaves and two fish.

"Five loaves and two fish.
It's only enough to fill
one dish!"

"This won't be enough
to feed the crowd," they said.
"There must be five thousand people!"

Jesus told his disciples to sit everyone down in groups. Jesus took the five loaves and two fish and thanked God for the food.

Then he divided the food into baskets
for each of the disciples.

The disciples shared the
food among the people.

Everyone ate as much
as they wanted.

CRUNCH!

MUNCH!

YUM!

After everyone
had eaten,
the disciples
collected
the baskets.

When they came back,
the twelve baskets were full of food!

They couldn't
believe their eyes.

Later, Jesus and his disciples
went down to the lake. They were
going to a town on the other side.

The disciples climbed into the boat.
Jesus stayed behind.

"You go on ahead,"
he told the disciples.
"I have something
I need to do first."

At last, the crowd went home. Jesus sat alone
on the mountain to pray.

Later that night,
Jesus looked out
over the lake.

SPLASH!

CRASH!

The boat was now far from the shore,
tossing this way and that.
The disciples were struggling to row the boat,
fighting against the wind and the waves.

It was still dark when the disciples saw
a white figure coming toward them.
They were terrified.

"It's a ghost!" they cried.

But it was Jesus,
walking on the water.

Jesus called to the disciples,
"Be brave! It's only me!"

"Lord, if it's you," Peter replied,
"tell me to come to you on the water."

"Come," Jesus said.

So Peter got out of the boat and
walked on the water toward Jesus.
But he was scared and began to sink.

Jesus held out his hand and caught Peter.
"Did you doubt that God would save you?" Jesus asked.

As they climbed back into the boat,
the wind died down.
The disciples were amazed.

"You really are the Son of God,"
they said to Jesus.

Next Steps

Look back through the book to find more to talk about and join in with.

* Copy the actions. Do the actions with the characters—put your hands together to pray; row the boat; pretend you are sinking in the water like Peter.

* Join in with the rhyme. Pause to encourage joining in with
"Five loaves and two fish.
It's only enough to fill one dish!"

* Count in fives and twos. Count two fish, two oars, five loaves, five sheep.

* Name the colors. What colors are in the boy's hat? Look back to spot the colors on other pages.

* All shapes and sizes. Look for big, middle-size, and small baskets and fish.

* Listen to the noisy crowd and storm. When you see the word on the page, point and make the sound—Crunch! Munch! Yum! Splash! Crash!

Now that you've read the story . . . what do you remember?

* Why was Jesus sad?
* How many people were in the crowd?
* What food did the disciples find?
* How many baskets of leftovers were there?
* Who walked on the water?
* How did people show they trusted God in the story?

What does the story tell us?
We should trust in God to give us all we need.

The
Last Supper

It was the Passover holiday. Jesus and his disciples were on their way to Jerusalem. Jesus sent two disciples ahead.

"Find me a young donkey," he told them.
The disciples found a young donkey and
brought it to Jesus.

Hee-haw!

As Jesus rode the donkey into Jerusalem, people came out to greet him. They spread palm leaves in his path and shouted for joy.

Hosanna!

"Hosanna, the king of the Jews has come
to save all of Jerusalem!"

Hosanna!

97

Jesus went to the temple to pray.
All around, people were changing
money and selling things.
Jesus lost his temper.

"This temple is for prayer," Jesus shouted,
"not for taking people's money."
He tipped over the tables.

Crash!

People cheered.
"Hosanna, the king
of the Jews has come
to save all of Jerusalem!"

Hosanna!

When the priests heard people cheering Jesus, they were afraid. They thought he was much too popular and powerful.

"We must get rid of him," the priests decided.
But Jerusalem was crowded for the holiday.
They didn't want any trouble.

"We will wait until the holiday is over,"
they agreed.
"Then we'll get him."

That evening, the disciples sat down to eat.
Jesus knew that this would be
their last supper together.

He began to wash
Peter's feet.

The disciples
were surprised.
Usually, servants
wash their
master's feet.

"What are you doing?"
asked Peter.

"I'm showing you that
I am God's servant,"
Jesus replied. "We must
all remember we are
God's servants."

While they ate their supper, Jesus said sadly,
"One of you will hand me over to the soldiers."
The disciples were shocked.

"You can't mean me!" they all said.

"Whoever shares this bowl with me," replied Jesus, "will betray me." Then Judas realized it was him.

Gulp!

"Is it me?" he asked. "You have said so," said Jesus.

While they were eating, Jesus picked up some bread.
He thanked God for the bread.

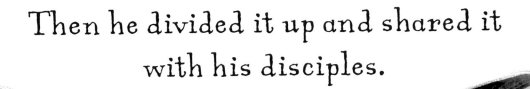

Then he divided it up and shared it with his disciples.

"Eat this," said Jesus. "This is my body."

Then Jesus took a cup of wine. He gave thanks for the wine and then passed it around.

"Drink this," he said.

"This is my blood, which is poured out to forgive your sins. This is the last drink of wine I will have in this world."

When they had finished their feast,
they went to the Mount of Olives.

"I am in trouble," said Jesus.

"You will all have to keep quiet and out of sight, or you'll be in trouble too."

"I'll never leave you," Peter replied.

"Peter, before the rooster crows in the morning," Jesus answered, "you will say you don't know me three times."

111

But Peter wouldn't believe it. "Even if I have to die, I will stick by you," he said.

All the disciples agreed that they would stand up for Jesus no matter what happened.

And while the disciples went to sleep, Jesus prayed.

Next Steps

Look back through the book to find more to talk about and join in with.

* Copy the actions. Do the actions with the characters—pretend to ride on a donkey; pretend to eat the bread; pretend to drink the wine.

* Join in with the rhyme. Pause to encourage joining in with
"Hosanna, the king of the Jews has come
to save all of Jerusalem!"

* Count twelve. Count the palm leaves, the doves in the temple, the disciples at the Last Supper.

* Name the colors. What colors are the disciples wearing? Look back to spot the colors on other pages.

* All shapes and sizes. Look for big, middle-size, and small candles.

* Listen to the sounds. When you see the word on the page, point and make the sound—Hee-haw! Hosanna! Crash! Gulp!

Now that you've read the story . . . what do you remember?

* What animal did Jesus ride into Jerusalem?
* What did people put on the ground in front of Jesus?
* Why did Jesus tip over the tables in the temple?
* What did Jesus say about the bread and wine that he shared?
* Who is going to hand Jesus over to the soldiers?
* How did Judas feel when he found out he was the one who would betray Jesus?

What does the story tell us?
Jesus was loved by the people but feared by the priests.

The Easter Story

It was a long, dark night. Jesus was in trouble. Some people said he was the king of the Jews—King Herod didn't like it.

While Jesus prayed, Peter, James, and John sat under the trees keeping watch.

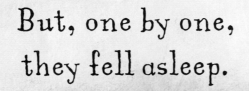

But, one by one,
they fell asleep.

Before sunrise, Jesus saw another disciple coming.
It was Judas, with a crowd carrying torches and
swords. Jesus woke the disciples.

"Hello, Master," said Judas,
and he kissed Jesus on the cheek.
Now the priests knew which man was Jesus.

Jesus was arrested. Peter swung his sword,
but Jesus told him not to fight.

Peter, James, and
John ran away.

Jesus was taken to the chief priest. Peter had
followed and was listening from a safe distance.
But someone spotted him.

"You were with Jesus," they said.
"No I wasn't," said Peter. "I don't know him."

Three times Peter said he didn't know Jesus,
just as Jesus had said he would.

Cock-a-doodle-doo! Then the rooster crowed, and
Peter cried because he hadn't
stood up for Jesus.

The priests took Jesus to Pilate, the Roman governor.
"Are you the king of the Jews?"
Pilate asked him. Jesus said nothing.

Pilate asked the crowd,
"What has he done?
He's hurt no one!"

But the crowd was angry.
"Who shall I let go?" asked Pilate. "Barabbas,
the murderer, or Jesus, king of the Jews?"

"Let Barabbas go!"
they cried.

Pilate was amazed, but
he let Barabbas go.

Boo!

The crowd made fun of Jesus as he
was taken to a hill called Calvary.
They put a crown of thorns on his head.

Boo!

Boo!

Jesus was nailed to a wooden cross between two thieves.
"If you are the Son of God," said the mean thief,
"why don't you save yourself?"

"What has he done? He's hurt no one!" said the kind thief.

At midday, the sky went dark.
The darkness lasted for three hours.

"God, forgive them," Jesus cried.
"They don't know what they are doing!"

At the same moment, the earth rumbled
and Jesus died.

A Roman soldier was
standing guard.
"He really was the
Son of God," he said.

That evening, a man called Joseph took Jesus' body to a stone tomb. He washed Jesus and dressed him in clean clothes. Then he rolled a heavy stone over the opening of the tomb.

Soldiers came to
guard the tomb.

All this time, Jesus' friends,
Mary Magdalene and Mary
from Galilee, were watching.

Two days later,
Mary Magdalene and
Mary from Galilee came
back to the tomb.

The soldiers were gone,
the stone was rolled back,
and the tomb was empty!

A shining angel said,
"Don't be afraid, Jesus is alive."

They ran quickly to tell the disciples.
But on the way, they met Jesus.

"Don't be afraid," said Jesus.
"I will meet the disciples in Galilee."

The disciples went to Galilee and waited. While they were talking, Jesus suddenly appeared. They were frightened!

"Why are you afraid?" asked Jesus. "It is me!" He showed them the marks on his hands and feet from the cross.

"Go and tell the world what I have taught you. Tell them they should be sorry for what they have done wrong. If other people do bad things you should forgive them."

Jesus led his disciples to
a place near Bethany.

He lifted up his hands
and blessed them.
Jesus left them and was
taken up into heaven.

The disciples went out
into the world.
They spread God's message,
just as Jesus had told them.

Next Steps

Look back through the book to find more to talk about and join in with.

* Copy the actions. Do the actions with the characters—pray; draw your sword; roll the heavy stone.

* Join in with the rhyme. Pause to encourage joining in with
"What has he done?
He's hurt no one!"

* Count in fours. Count Jesus, Peter, James, and John, count four torches, count the three women and John by the cross, count four doves.

* Name the colors. What color clothes can you see in the crowd? Look back to spot the colors on other pages.

* All shapes and sizes. Look for big, middle-size, and small trees.

* Listen to the noisy rooster. When you see the word on the page, point and make the sound—Cock-a-doodle-doo! Boo!

Now that you've read the story . . . what do you remember?

* Who led the crowd to Jesus?
* How many times did Peter say that he didn't know Jesus?
* What did the crowd put on Jesus' head?
* How did Jesus die?
* Where was Jesus buried?
* Who found out first that Jesus was alive?

What does the story tell us?
Jesus showed us that we should forgive other people, not blame them.